Andrew Jackson

Populist President

Peg Robinson

Cavendish Square

New York

Published in 2019 by Cavendish Square Publishing, LLC
243 5th Avenue, Suite 136, New York, NY 10016

Copyright © 2019 by Cavendish Square Publishing, LLC

First Edition

Library of Congress Cataloging-in-Publication Data

Names: Robinson, Peg, author.
Title: Andrew Jackson : populist president / Peg Robinson.
Description: First edition. | New York : Cavendish Square, 2019 |
Series: Hero or villain? Claims and counterclaims |
Includes bibliographical references and index.| Audience: Grades 7-12.
Identifiers: LCCN 2017052048 (print) | LCCN 2017052233 (ebook) |
ISBN 9781502635266 (library bound) | ISBN 9781502635280 (pbk.) | ISBN 9781502635273 (ebook)
Subjects: LCSH: Jackson, Andrew, 1767-1845--Juvenile literature. |
Presidents--United States--Biography--Juvenile literature.
Classification: LCC E382 (ebook) | LCC E382 .R63 2019 (print) | DDC 973.5/6092 [B] --dc23
LC record available at https://lccn.loc.gov/2017052048

Editorial Director: David McNamara
Editor: Michael Spitz
Copy Editor: Rebecca Rohan
Associate Art Director: Amy Greenan
Designer: Amy Greenan/Christina Shults
Production Coordinator: Karol Szymczuk
Photo Research: J8 Media

CONTENTS

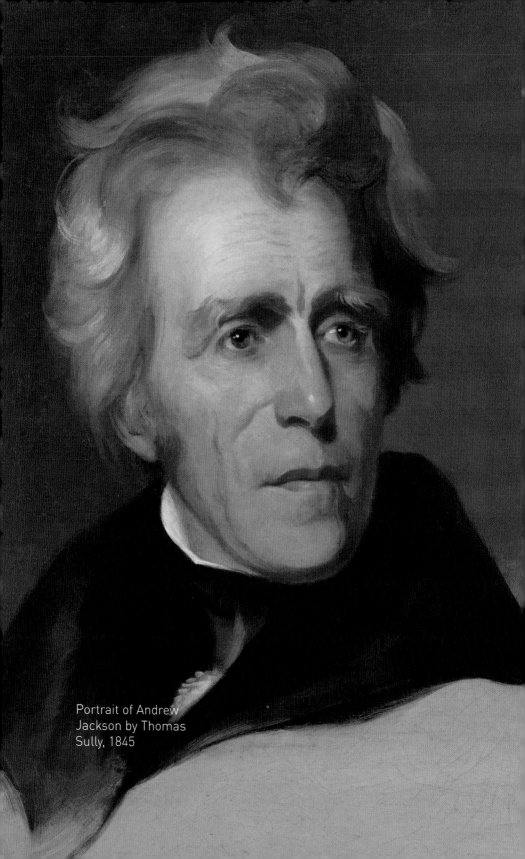

Portrait of Andrew Jackson by Thomas Sully, 1845

Andrew Jackson, the Man Who Defined an Era

Andrew Jackson was called "Old Hickory" and "The People's President." He was loved and honored as a soldier, a statesman, a nation-builder, and a man who defended what many people of his era considered the core principles of the new American nation. He was a loyal husband, a bold general, and a generous friend but a vicious enemy. He served his nation as a judge, a general, a congressman, a senator, and as president.

His life, from his birth in a log cabin in frontier territory until his death as an honored and revered figure of a growing nation, was quickly woven into the United States' myth of its own character—so much so that for generations to come, public servants drew on the legends and tropes of Jackson's life to bolster their own careers. Everyone wanted to be born in a frontier log cabin. Everyone wanted to fight in the Revolutionary War and the War of 1812, and conquer much of Spanish-owned Florida. Everyone wanted to be what was called back then an Indian Fighter. Everyone wanted to be part of the Jacksonian moment. They wanted to represent the sentiment of "one man, one vote." Every American politician wanted to be seen as a populist, even if he wasn't one. Every candidate hoped to "cleanse government of corruption." Everyone wanted to be both "of the people" and "of the elite" at the same time.

Jackson managed to represent everything the newborn United States admired in a man, and in itself. He was bold, rugged, and hot-tempered, but canny. He was fiercely patriotic. He believed in the union of the states and believed they must abide together, in spite of their many differences. He defined an era that sought to make the abolitionist lie down with the slave owner in good faith and mutual respect. He defined a culture that sought to combine the robust, freewheeling, adaptive traits of the frontier with the restrained, educated, refined expectations of the oldest colonies, aspiring to the highest standards of the cities of the Old World.

His accomplishments in his lifetime were outstanding and largely admired by the people of his time. He fought Native Americans in war and won. He fought them in law, too, and not only won, but forced them out of European-held territory. It was seen at the time as a brilliant and forceful victory for American settlement but is now seen as a genocidal tragedy. As a soldier, and later an officer, he

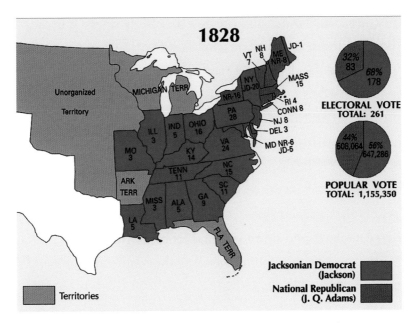

This map shows the results of the 1828 presidential election.

fought the British twice, in the American Revolution and in the War of 1812, scoring a major victory in retaking and defending New Orleans. He wrested Floridian territory from the Spanish.

He expanded the voting franchise, granting the vote to all white American men, destroying the monopoly of the old pseudoaristocracy of moneyed landowners. He founded the Democratic Party (which was then pro-slavery), securing what became our current two-party system after a long struggle with the hopes of the original Founders, who had wanted to avoid a party-run government. As president, he successfully increased trade, improving the economy. He fought corruption and nepotism in the federal government. He negotiated a real, if short-lived, peace between the

Southern slave states and the Northern free states. It avoided the problems involved in the nullification movement, in which states hoped to use "states' rights" as an argument for ignoring federal power.

Much of that record, so shining in the eyes of his contemporaries, is tainted in the eyes of modern students of history. He believed firmly in conquest, he accepted slavery and worked to preserve that institution, and he held racial beliefs that may currently be considered deplorable. He was fierce, violent, and often vulgar. His principles do not match the people of the present as well as they matched the people of his own age.

Was Andrew Jackson a hero or a villain? The truth is complicated, and the final judgment is a matter of personal beliefs and principles. Even in his own time, there were many who disagreed with his politics and despised his personal behavior. Those of us in the present must judge Jackson warily, trying to balance the norms and ideals of his period with those of our own time. It's a challenge. The virtues Jackson demonstrated are jarring to modern eyes.

The West Frontier

States and Territories of the United States of America
1795 to June 1 1796

Political geography of North America, 1795–1796

Many modern people think of the "frontier" as the far
west of the North American continent and don't think
anything east of the Mississippi counts as such. At
the time of Andrew Jackson's birth, the area known to
European settlers had not yet reached the interior of
the continent. By the time Jackson left office, the United
States' holdings had expanded to the Mississippi and
farther, with the frontier beginning to resemble those
areas we now picture when we hear that term.

When Jackson was a child and a young man,
however, the frontier included much of what we
currently think of as "colonial America." He was born

Territorial growth of the United States over time

Andrew Jackson: Populist President

in the Waxhaws area in the Piedmont, an area that was later divided between North and South Carolina. He came of age and became a lawyer in what was then the Western District of North Carolina, which was later classified as Tennessee. By the time he first served the nation as a Congressman, the shift was made, and the man licensed as a lawyer in North Carolina became a Congressman of Tennessee.

The frontier at the time was undergoing rapid change and would continue to do so throughout Andrew Jackson's life. The shift from Native American–held territory to European-held territory to full member state of the United States was quick, and legal and moral norms were fluid. It is impossible to fairly judge Jackson's life without understanding that he grew up in a world undergoing constant change, with standards being invented and discarded faster than anyone could easily track.

America's independence from Great Britain began in 1776.

History

Most historical figures are defined by their eras. They may have an effect on the world, but the effect is limited. A few, however, mark their era so deeply that they define it. Andrew Jackson was a pivotal figure in his time. His actions as a lawyer, soldier, congressman, senator, and most of all as the seventh president of the United States, changed the world as much as the American Revolution. The United States, as we understand it, draws heavily on the Jacksonian period—though modern Americans are often more horrified and offended by Jacksonian norms and beliefs than approving. Jackson's period exemplified many of the things Americans find embarrassing about the nation's past. Jackson's beliefs and choices often look as disgusting to modern eyes as they looked admirable to the eyes of his own generation.

When you study Andrew Jackson and his life, you are studying the evolution of a nation from thirteen colonies to a continent. You are studying the slave-based economy of the South, in conflict with the free-labor North. You are studying the forced eviction and attempted genocide of the Native American population, and the beginning of a policy in which the United States regarded all treaties with Native Americans as nonbinding on the side of the federal government, while completely binding on the many tribes who signed those treaties. The period demonstrated the radical legal differences between the frontier territories and the older, established coastal communities. It showed how quickly the border of the frontier swept west, moving from the chain of the Appalachians to the Mississippi and beyond in less than one lifetime. It showed the real cultural divorce between the expectations of a "civilized" Europe, and those of a radicalized, democratic, new nation.

America, from the time of the revolution onward, was a new world being born. Andrew Jackson was a towering figure who helped define that new world.

Jackson was born in 1767 (before the revolution) in what was then a territory of North Carolina, though it was reclassified as part of Tennessee during his lifetime. He was the son of Scots-Irish immigrants, who came to the New World to settle. He and his family took part in the Revolutionary War. Young Andrew took part in the fighting, experienced the bloodshed, and was ultimately orphaned in the war. In spite of that, he went on to become a respected professional. He married Rachel Donelson Robards under circumstances that later came back to haunt the couple. He served his nation repeatedly. When he at last became president, he brought his lifetime of experiences with him, from the Native American–occupied frontier of his youth, through the war against the British, to the fast-changing culture of a frontier becoming a civilized state.

Andrew Jackson achieved many great things, but he also performed other actions and espoused many beliefs we now consider less admirable. Whether we are discussing the Jacksonian swing from appointed representation to a presumption of one man, one vote, or are considering the tragedy of the Trail of Tears, there's a lot to cover. It is hard for modern Americans to read about a time when our country favored expansion through conquest, genocidal cleansing of Native populations, and forced slavery of black African natives that was not only accepted, but admired.

It is, however, unavoidably true: America in the late 1700s and early 1800s accepted all these things as both normal and admirable. The assumptions were not universal, but they were common. Those who disagreed were not only few— those few were often as offensive in their own opinions. Those who opposed slavery, for example, often favored forced repatriation of former slaves back to Africa. People who favored fair treatment of Native populations often favored mandatory extinction of the cultures, if not the people. The desired goal was to establish a European-based democratic nation on democratic principles. At that time, there was no ideal of a "melting pot," much less a multicultural patchwork. More precisely, the patchwork was assumed to exist on a regional basis and to be dealt with by regional norms—and the European culture was expected to dominate in all cases.

It is said that the past is a different country. In the case of the differences between the modern USA and that of Andrew Jackson's past, that's true, and Andrew Jackson only made it more true.

Colonialism and Imperialism; Slavery and Genocide

To understand the nation Jackson grew up in, it's important to focus on a few points. First, the United States was still colonial. In winning its freedom from England against all reasonable expectations, the United States became hyperaware of itself as entirely separate from England. There was an obsession with the United States having its own self-identity.

Understanding the politics of the United States during the Jacksonian era demands recognition of this obsession. Americans as a whole were concerned with continuing to cut the ties and define the differences between themselves and the Old World. They were also concerned with establishing their country as one with a destiny. Given the number of religiously committed people in the United States at that time, it was no wonder that their idea of a destined nation was colored by two comparisons. The first was to Rome—the greatest empire in the eyes of that period. The other was the nation of Israel, and in particular the city of Jerusalem.

These were powerful and meaningful comparisons to those who settled the country. Even atheists and nonbelievers of every background understood these two comparisons. They proved to be effective in establishing two roles we both emulated and rejected.

Rome was the benchmark empire for most of the Western world at that time. At its height, it had ruled the majority of the west, from the Atlantic and Mediterranean coasts to the steppes and India. Americans wanted to equal Rome's capacity for conquest, in particular conquest of new territory and "lesser" people. While they disliked being under the colonial rule of England, they approved of imperialism and colonialism when it was the United States colonizing other territories. That was especially true in regards to what our ancestors considered land occupied by "savages." In that situation, the United States was convinced it had a role many considered not just given by God, but decreed as a necessity and backed by divine aid. Euro-Americans were like the ancient Israelites entering their promised land.

The United States was far less comfortable when it came to attempts to colonialize lands previously held by countries that the US considered "civilized." Enthusiasm dropped further away from the continental, contiguous United States. Americans of the time saw it as a form of minding their own business: they had an entire half-continent assigned to them that was their proper concern. Americans would plow

Greco-Roman style marble bust of Andrew Jackson by Hiram
Powers, 1839.

their own assigned field and leave the rest to take care of themselves. Many men and women, including the Founders, considered it an American virtue. George Washington himself wrote:

> The great rule of conduct for us, in regard to foreign nations, is in extending our commercial relations to have as little political connection as possible ... Why, by interweaving our destiny with that of any part of Europe, entangle our peace and prosperity in the toils of European ambition, rivalships, interest, humor, or caprice? ... It is our true policy to steer clear of permanent alliances with any portion of the foreign world.

This touched on two aspects of American identity. As a people, Americans saw themselves as separate and unentangled in a military or political sense. This divorced the nation from the aristocracies of the Old Countries of Europe and most of the world. They saw themselves as a nation of businessmen, merchants, and farmers, engaged in the very "trade" that much of European high society considered lowly and beneath the interest of the upper classes. Both were points of pride. Americans of the era wanted the nation and its citizens to show the virtues they associated with common tradesmen and farmers. They should be thrifty, determined, competitive, and willing to fight for their dominance, but they should not look for greater glories than were sent by a

Appointment to the Senate

At the time of Andrew Jackson's appointment to the Senate, the position of senator was not gained by vote, but by appointment from the state legislature. This was the method of selection chosen by the Founders in the Constitution.

Over time, that method became less and less popular. Americans felt an ever-stronger conviction that the individual vote was a crucial element of self-government, a sentiment that first gained power and popularity during Andrew Jackson's career. From that time, when populism first became a powerful force in American politics, until 1913, when the Seventeenth Amendment was passed, making the position of senator an electoral rather than an appointed position, Americans were able to see the limits imposed by permitting the state legislators to choose their senators.

Besides a simple objection to being deprived of the opportunity to choose, Americans came to realize that the senatorial position was held for much longer than that of a congressman. Individual senators were often so much more powerful that they dominated politics to the point of blocking needed change. The in-state battles to appoint such powerful players became hostile as the Civil War approached, and the Republicans and

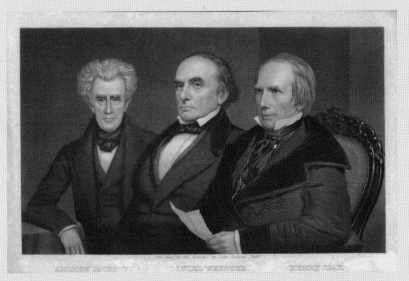

Andrew Jackson, Daniel Webster and Henry Clay were important US senators. Engraved portrait by John Sartain.

Democrats of the day fought to gain advantage through the number of free states versus slave states. After the Civil War, in-state battles over the appointment of a senator became still more contentious, with regular accusations of the ways different factions within politics were gaming the system.

Pressure to reform the method of selection began as early as 1826, even before Andrew Jackson's first term as president. During the upswing in populism during that period, there were calls for direct voting for senators. At that time, the push failed. It took the dysfunction of the following seventy-five years to gather enough support to push through a constitutional amendment.

divine maker. They hoped they were not too good to work hard or take gambles on their own good fortune. What they won in combat or in trade was theirs to develop without guilt, but their primary concern should be their own assigned challenge. In the territories assigned them, they could and should be relentless and remorseless, pursuing victory in the face of all challenges. Americans imagined themselves building a divine city on a hill, demonstrating faith and good works as good Christians, and equally demonstrating tenacity, ferocity, and guile as good businessmen.

These beliefs were entangled with complicated, often amoral beliefs about the value of non-European people. The history of these complicated attitudes is long, but Americans' beliefs about themselves as a nation were woven into their beliefs about slavery, and their beliefs about the worth and the destiny of the Native American peoples. It is enough to know that for many people in the newly created United States, the destruction of the Native population and the maintenance of the slave-based economy of the Southern states was not only acceptable, but virtuous and desirable. Those who were considered good people often also killed and abused Natives and kept slaves. Many of their fellow citizens thought more highly of them for doing so.

Frontier Law and Culture

When studying this time period, it is also important to recognize the difference between the laws and standards of established cities and communities in the eastern portions of the new states, and the culture and legal expectations of

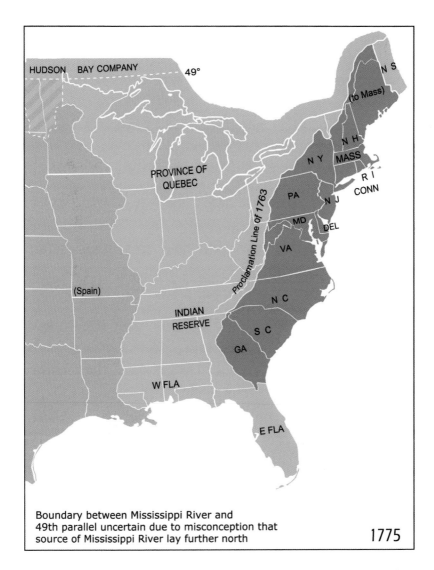

Boundary between Mississippi River and
49th parallel uncertain due to misconception that
source of Mississippi River lay further north

1775

Territorial distribution of eastern North America between England,
Spain, France, and Native Territory in 1775

denizens of the frontier. The two were often worlds apart, for many reasons.

First was desperation—or the lack of desperation. The established communities had passed their desperate years, a century and more before. The cities and townships of the Eastern Seaboard seldom had to fear armed attack by Native American forces, starvation through failed crops, or death via the elements. Failed outposts like Roanoke were a thing of the past in the civilized lands surrounding major cities like Boston, Philadelphia, and Jamestown. They had the time, security, established governmental systems, infrastructure, and wealth to try to match the best "civilization" could offer.

The fear of massacre, famine, drought, plague, and extreme weather still haunted the frontier. Neither the social infrastructure nor the legal system had been created yet. In a world where transportation was slow and the territory dangerous, a family or group of families who went into the western wilderness could be lost without a trace. Native populations, increasingly angry and afraid as Europeans swept into their lands, were capable of resistance, both on an individual level and as armed tribes and nations. While the wild frontier ensured that no burgeoning family in the East needed to fear that their younger sons and daughters might not own their own land, it also placed those sons and daughters at risk.

Many settlers were European immigrants. That, too, added to the difference between communities and social standards. Europe was full of land-hungry commoners coming directly from a culture in which landowners and only landowners had a lot of political power or social status.

It is commonplace in modern history to recognize the powerful relationship Native Americans had with their land. It is less commonplace to realize that, for immigrants coming from Europe, the chance to become a landowner was the difference between near-serf status and entry into the security and pride of rank, and the stability of owning the basis of their own living. It carried religious meanings of stewardship and secular meanings of high status and security. These immigrants had powerful feelings about land. They had the chance to own, develop, and tend it. It was not a situation of one culture that held land dearly and another that merely treated it as a sort of trade item. It was a case of two radically different cultures and economies, both treasuring land in entirely different ways. Both sides were offended by the way their different cultures dealt with land and land rights. Neither side had the education, training, and experience to fully understand the other's perspective, and both were desperate enough to enter into outright war to defend their own system. That was the result.

While there may have been some people in the new United States who wanted to see justice done to the Native Americans, few wanted to return land to them, and fewer were to be found on the frontier. Native Americans saw Europeans stealing land long considered holy in their own right and shared in common by many people; Europeans saw Native communities, in keeping the wilderness, as wasting land. In that era, wasting land was as wrong as polluting it is to us today. To the settlers, Native Americans were keeping land that could give millions of people homes, farms, mills, factories, towns, cities, roads, mines—they were keeping that gift from God unused and wasted. Add that offense to many other biased disagreements, and the region was left with Native Americans who had no sympathy for invading swarms of settlers, and settlers with no sympathy at all for the Native Americans.

It was in this period that the cultural belief of "the only good Indians were dead Indians" began to take root. More and more European people were born in America, or sailed to her shores, wanting more and more land. More and more Native Americans resisted. Necessity was forcing both sides to become more and more aggressive in their approach to settlement.

In this situation, fighters were in high standing. Men and women who were as skilled with a gun as they were with a plow or a loom were precious to their homesteads and their communities. Many of the people coming to America were already trained in a similar mindset. At that time, the first flow of Scots-Irish settlers came into the United States, many of them moving directly to the frontier to claim land and start farms and plantations.

The Life and Times of Young Andrew Jackson

As said, Andrew Jackson was born to Scots-Irish settlers who had previously lived in County Antrim, Ireland. The

Irish Jacksons had been successful, rising to the status of educated lower tradesmen and gentry, holding their own in the hostile country. At the time, they would have been considered part of the Anglo-Protestant Ascendancy. These were Protestant families that moved in from Scottish and English communities to colonize and control rebellious Catholic Ireland. The Jacksons and Hutchinses (Andrew's mother's family), however, were Presbyterian, putting them at odds with the reigning Anglican faction among the Ascendancy. The younger Jacksons chose to follow in the steps of other family members and to seek their own good fortune further abroad. Andrew Jackson Sr. and his pregnant wife, Elizabeth Hutchins Jackson, arrived with their two elder sons, Hugh and Robert. They migrated quickly to the frontier lands, then held as part of colonial South Carolina, in an area called the Waxhaws. They joined a settlement that included three sisters and two brothers of the couple.

Andrew Sr. died in an accident a mere three weeks prior to Elizabeth giving birth to Andrew Jr., who would grow up without a father. His norms would be the norms of the frontier. His culture would be that of Scots-Irish frontier men and women. Elizabeth would do what she could to raise her boys among relatives, choosing to live with an aunt and uncle in the region. Her son was educated by two local priests.

Revolutionary War

The family remained stable and hung on during the Revolutionary War. The entire family fought on the side

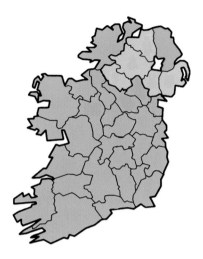

This map shows Ireland, with Northern Ireland in pink and County Antrim in bright green.

of the rebels against England. Hugh, the eldest brother, fought in the 1779 Battle of Stono Ferry, where he died of heat exhaustion. After the Waxhaws Massacre in 1780, Elizabeth convinced her two remaining sons to practice with the local militia. They were young enough to be chosen as couriers. These young messengers, Native-born to the arena they fought in, would run messages between groups of militiamen, darting through the woodlands and fields carrying critical military communiques. The two brothers served as couriers during the Battle of Hanging Rock in 1780. They were captured by the British in early winter of 1781. Both brothers refused to be used as servants by the British officers during their imprisonment and were beaten and scarred for their rebellion. During their time as prisoners, they were ill-fed to the point of near starvation, and they contracted smallpox. Andrew developed a lifelong hatred of the British during that period.

His mother, Elizabeth, obtained their release in early spring of 1781. She arrived on foot to collect the boys, and the three set out walking on the return home. Robert, however, died a few days later, on April 27. Elizabeth stayed to nurse Andrew to health, then volunteered to work as a nurse with prisoners of war suffering from cholera, pent up on two ships held captive in Charleston harbor. She contracted the disease while serving her patients, died, and was buried in an unmarked grave.

Andrew was an orphan at this point, with his parents and both siblings dead. He still had claim to protection and help from his aunts and uncles in the Waxhaw region of the territory. At fourteen, he was old enough to be seen as more of a man than a child by the community standards of the era. He would have been expected to pull his own weight in the community.

He continued his education for a time, then went on to teach, having chosen to leave training as a saddler. As a teacher, he boarded with local families, freeing him from dependence on his surviving relations. Eventually, he chose to leave the area and go to Salisbury, North Carolina, where he took up a law apprenticeship with a local lawyer. Upon qualifying for the bar and becoming a lawyer himself, he became a prosecutor for the Western District of North Carolina—an area that would very soon be recognized as part of the new state of Tennessee. This position led him to move to Nashville, Tennessee. He had gained his first profession, taken his first public office, fought his first duel, and bought his first slave. Soon, he was to marry his first and only wife.

His marriage to Rachel Donelson Robards was a minor scandal at the time and became a major scandal during the course of his political life. Frontier law and culture clashed with "civilized" standards of the older, established communities, and the ever-more-citified standards of the changing frontier.

Rachel Donelson Robards was married … unhappily married. At that time and in that place, the effort and cost of obtaining a divorce was extreme. In frontier communities, it was not uncommon for an unhappy couple to simply take matters into their own hands, separating with no intention of rejoining as a couple. Rachel apparently chose a version of this form of divorce. There are varied versions of Andrew and Rachel's marriage, an event obscured by both the lack of clear records during the period and of manufactured slanders later in their lives. What remains clear is that Andrew and Rachel returned to Nashville after a half-year absence, presenting themselves as husband and wife—and that Rachel's prior husband objected. There are claims that they had believed Mr. Robards to have already divorced Rachel. There are claims of an official marriage out of the territory. What is certain is that in the face of Robards's protests, they proceeded with an official, legal divorce.

They were never free of their reputation for adultery, bigamy, and low morals. The clash between cultural standards remained with them for the rest of their lives and may have sped up Rachel's eventual death.

MRS. ANDREW JACKSON.

This portrait, printed and distributed on a cigarette card, shows Andrew Jackson's wife, Rachel.

Distribution of Americans of Scots-Irish descent

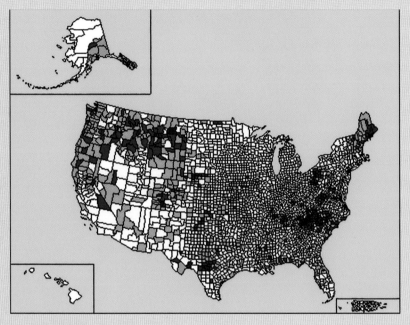

A more modern depiction of areas with Americans of Scots-Irish descent. Red indicated higher concentrations.

The Scots-Irish culture had faced centuries of conflict, first in the Highlands of Scotland, during the Jacobean wars, and then in Northern Ireland, as Protestants attempted to colonize Catholic Ireland. For generations, their culture had valued the "hard" man or woman who could ply a trade, use weapons, and fight rather than sit peacefully. The ideal person was loyal to his or her kin and community and hostile to all outsiders. They brought their endurance, their close family ties, their independence and pride, and their passionate disregard for outsider's rules with them. Andrew Jackson was born of a Scots-Irish couple and grew up among settlers. He lived up to their values and their standards.

On the frontier, law was seldom as important as community acceptance, and "rights" were a matter of strength, courage, and the ability to get away with breaking rules and limits. That was not just a matter of pride and rebelliousness. There were so few lawyers, so few judges, so few places that were even sure where to look for authority, that settlers were making it up as they went along. This would be of special importance in regards to Andrew Jackson's marriage to Rachel Donelson Robards.

Early Years of Public Service

During the following years, prior to his election as president, Andrew Jackson worked as a private citizen, a businessman, and a public servant. As a businessman, he took part in land speculation and the development of settlements. His land speculation was based on the open choice to purchase lands reserved by treaty for the Cherokee and to resell the property to white owners. He also purchased land and properties for himself, starting in 1803. Two years later, he bought the property that was to become his family plantation, the Hermitage, outside Nashville, Tennessee. The Hermitage was a slave-based plantation specializing in growing cotton.

As a public servant, he first served as an elected member of the constitutional convention that established the new state of Tennessee's state constitution. The following year, he was elected as Tennessee's only congressman. A year later, he was appointed to the position of senator of Tennessee. He resigned that role after one year. He then went on to serve as an officer in Tennessee's militia.

GENERAL ANDREW JACKSON.

Portrait of General Andrew Jackson, after the Battle of New Orleans, taken from an etching by Asher Brown Durand, 1828

General Andrew Jackson led the American troops against the British in the Battle of New Orleans.

The Facts

I t was during these later years that Andrew Jackson's most remembered actions took place. During this time, he grew his plantation in size and scope, buying more slaves and expanding his fortunes. He served first in the war against the Creek Indians (as they were then called) and later in the War of 1812. He ran for president in 1824, lost, then won in 1828. As president, he changed the conception of the powers of office put in place by the Founders, fought government corruption, and in the process, challenged the balance of power between the branches of government. He signed the Indian Removal Act of 1830 into law and then implemented it vigorously. He overturned tariffs that were legally voted into law but unpopular with the Southern states. The South imported more foreign goods than the Northern states and thus had to pay more tariffs. He attacked the national bank created by Alexander Hamilton and the system of paper money. He developed a response to the nullification strategy advanced by the Southern states to overthrow federal power and protect the slave-based economic system.

Each of these things was considered controversial in its time and in modern times. Each brought Jackson both praise and condemnation. To this day, any of these topics can and will raise a powerful response in the public forum. There are still people who consider Jackson a hero as well as a villain for his actions. Let's take a closer look at some of those actions.

The Hermitage: A Slave Plantation

Andrew Jackson bought the first portion of land for what would eventually become his plantation, the Hermitage, in 1804. Many of the details of the property and its use are contested. One source suggests the original property was 420 acres (170 hectares); another insists it was 640 acres (259 ha). Some think the Jacksons first occupied the property with only two slaves in their household. Another believes they owned nine. All agree that it was a cotton plantation purchased from Nathaniel Hays, a friend of Jackson's, and that they used a slave workforce from the start. These sources also agree that it grew in installments over the years, having reached approximately 1,000 acres (405 ha) at the time of Andrew Jackson's death. At no time was it ever not a slave-supported business, nor is there any indication Jackson intended to manumit his slaves or expected his heirs to do so.

The Hermitage boasts a classical façade.

"Uncle Albert's Cabin," a slave cabin at the Hermitage

There are arguments that the slaves were kindly kept, based on the testimony of Hannah Jackson, one of Andrew and Rachel's most trusted household slaves. This testimony was gathered by James Parton, a historical writer presenting a three-volume biographical work on Jackson at the start of the Civil War. Knowing that the issue of slavery must be addressed, he found Hannah still living at the Hermitage. He recorded her assessments of Jackson. She stated he was "more a father to us than a master" and assured Parton that the household slaves were treated like family—if not as equals. That testimony conflicts with records of the time describing whippings and beatings and the separation of families. It's not easy to determine if Parton's reporting was accurate, honest, and unaltered.

What can be said is that the Hermitage was a successful plantation in its day, growing in size and in population, allowing the Jacksons an increasingly comfortable lifestyle. What started as a log fortress ended as a Greek revival mansion surrounded by acres of cotton fields and kept running with as many as 110 slaves at the time of Jackson's death and probate process. This was not considered shameful in that time and place but was instead the mark of Jackson's rising fortunes and increasing respectability. Tennessee was a slave state. Its residents believed in slavery as a right and a necessity. Jackson showed no sign of disagreeing.

During its history, the Hermitage was left under the care of both Hannah Jackson, who was trusted to manage the basic housekeeping and upkeep of the home, and of

Andrew Jackson Jr. Andrew Jackson Jr. was a son adopted from Rachel's brother and sister-in-law. It's unclear whether he was adopted due to ill health on the part of his birth mother, to reduce financial and family pressure caused by an extra and unplanned-for infant, or to provide Rachel and Jackson with a child. It is recorded that Jackson loved Andrew Jr., and all of his adopted or mentored family. Andrew Jackson Jr., however, proved a bad manager for the Hermitage, allowing it to fall into disrepair during his father's absence and after his father's death.

The Creek War and the Battle of Horseshoe Bend

The Creek War was fought between the Creek Confederacy (a tribal-alliance nation not unlike the Cherokee or the Iroquois) and white settlers. The war was precipitated by the increasing pressure on Native American territories and communities by the also increasing European-American settlements. It was a war with many factions, dividing the Creek nation and pitting those who wished to battle the European invaders against several different European governments and empires.

The war started as a Native American civil war between factions of Creek. Creek territory occupied a space that included parts of the Carolinas (under US rule), Florida (under Spanish rule), and Louisiana (under French rule until the Louisiana Purchase transferred it to US control in 1803). The tribe was being torn apart by three nations, each land-greedy and determined to establish territories for their settlers. At one time, the Creek Confederacy had

A popular etching of the Battle of Horseshoe Bend

successfully used the conflicts between the European nations to control the situation, pitting one invader against the other. The shifts occurring in the region after the establishment of the United States had thrown that balance out, leaving the invaders to disrupt the Native American nation. Much of the conflict arose from problems with the economics of the Creek, trapped halfway between traditional Native American trade economies and an economy increasingly dependent on American and European goods. Among the factions in the Creek nation, the Red Sticks were powerfully resistant to European influence. They felt they had no choice but to try to drive the Europeans from Native lands and territories.

The Red Stick leaders were inspired by the rebellion and the religious passion of Tecumseh and Tenskwatawa of the Shawnee, to the northwest. They were further supported by visits and advice from those war chiefs. The religious elements quickly spread among the Creek. Soon the Red Sticks began their rebellion, only to have it quickly involve US military forces.

For the United States, the official start of the Creek War came on July 21, 1813. The war lasted until August 9, 1814, when General Andrew Jackson, victorious from the Battle of Horseshoe Bend, forced the two headmen of Upper and Lower Creek township to sign the Treaty of Fort Jackson. His military victory ended Creek hopes of winning back their own lands.

The battle itself occurred over a single day, on March 27, 1813. General Jackson, commanding a mixed force of United States forces and allied Native American warriors,

A portrait of the Creek war leader Menawa by Charles
Bird King, 1825

broke through the defenses of the Red Sticks, led by their war chief, Menawa. The Red Stick position had been considered impregnable by its occupants. They had settled on a place surrounded on three sides by a looping bend of the Tallapoosa River, in Tennessee. The fourth side was blocked with heavy, strong fortifications. They were well-armed, well-manned, and prepared for combat.

In spite of that, Jackson's greater forces overwhelmed them in the end. Jackson sent his junior officer, General John Coffee, to take a group of Native American allies over the southern branch of the Tallapoosa, allowing them to circle around to the back of the Red Sticks. The group crossed the river while the Red Sticks were kept busy and distracted by Jackson's own frontal attack on their barricades. The end was complete and bloody. Jackson's forces killed the Native Americans without mercy. Jackson lost less than fifty men; the Red Shirts lost over eight hundred out of one thousand or more.

The battle became one of Andrew Jackson's more famous victories. He was seen as a hero by millions of Americans who had feared a new and organized Native American war brewing on their western flank. The possibility of alliances joining in resistance to US settlements distressed people who feared Native American massacre, and those who merely feared losing their chance at Native American lands.

In a previous battle of the Creek War, the Battle of the Tallushatchee, Jackson discovered an orphaned infant boy among the Native Americans. Rather than kill the baby, return it to its people, or give it to some other family to raise, Jackson adopted the Creek child himself and raised him as his own. The boy was named Lyncoya. By all reports, he was loved and supported, with Jackson intending to send him to West Point when he came of age. Unfortunately, Lyncoya contracted smallpox at the age of sixteen and died before attaining adulthood.

The Battle of New Orleans

If the Battle of Horseshoe Bend was Jackson's great military defeat of the Native Americans, the Battle of New Orleans, which helped end the War of 1812 as decisively as he had ended the Creek War, was his victory against the British. Where the Battle of Horseshoe Bend took only a single day,

Painting of the Battle of New Orleans, by Edward Percy Moran, 1910

the Battle of New Orleans lasted over a month, continuing from December 14, 1814 to January 18, 1815.

Jackson, by then a major general, was the commanding officer overseeing the battle. He was up against what would normally have been a superior force, under the command of Admiral Alexander Cochrane and General Edward Pakenham.

New Orleans had been American territory since the Louisiana Purchase in 1803. It was a tempting point of attack for the British—it was seated at the mouth of America's greatest river, the Mississippi. It provided the British with a clear line of advance from the Gulf of Mexico all the way up the continent until just short of the Great Lakes, with an enormous network of associated tributary rivers. The Mississippi granted access to the entire heart of the new continent. Further, New Orleans was not yet assimilated into the new nation. Loyalties of New Orleans residents, formerly under French rule, allowed the possibility of forming willing alliances against the new US overlords. The port favored the British navy. The wilderness between the established territories of the United States and the new port city put the US forces at a disadvantage. Admiral Cochrane and General Pakenham had reason for confidence.

The battle was fought after the British had officially given up and after the signing of the Treaty of Ghent. Due to communication difficulties of the period, however, none of the combatants knew they were no longer at war. The battle was fought in good faith by forces who believed the outcome of the war might hang on their actions. Word of the treaty did not arrive until January 18. By then, the British had retreated from the fray. They didn't surrender but were unable to continue their engagement. Victory had already been in Jackson's hands; the news of the treaty merely ensured the combat would end.

The battle began on December 12, when a British fleet of sixty ships attempted to take control of the port and the adjoining Lakes Pontchartrain and Borgne. The attack was resisted by resident soldiers and sailors, but the British succeeded in gaining access to Lake Borgne. From there, they had access to New Orleans, where they established a garrison under the command of General John Keane, and proceeded to try to secure the territory. Keane headed up the Mississippi, intending to surprise American forces up the river, choosing to camp at Lacoste's Plantation.

Major General Jackson only heard about the attack on December 23. He brought his troops down the river and attacked Keane and his men by night. The attack was a draw at best, and at worst, a tactical victory for the British, who held their encampment. The entire drive of the campaign was turned aside, and the British were no longer free to pour up the Mississippi River unchecked. In the remaining days of the battle, the British did not win any victories sufficient to maintain their campaign's momentum. By the time the main British forces arrived, the Americans were entrenched and settled in for a long fight. The British enjoyed only one major victory during the entire battle, and that was not enough to prevent the eventual retreat of the British forces. When news of the Treaty of Ghent finally arrived, Major General

Etching of General Andrew Jackson, in celebration of the Battle of New Orleans

Jackson had already secured and stabilized the city of New Orleans against forces far greater than his own.

Election to the Presidency

Andrew Jackson first ran for the presidency in 1824. He lost to John Quincy Adams. The two men were passionately at odds. John Quincy Adams was the son of the nation's second president, John Adams. He had many of the virtues and flaws of his father. Like his father, he was a private man with a preference for private study and activities over social interactions. He was as close as the Northeast had to an "aristocrat," the heir to one of the great founding figures of the nation. He was a diplomat, a politician, and a statesman. He was conservative in the opinions of the people of the time. Where Jackson was a wholehearted conqueror, convinced of the value and need of aggressive expansion, Adams was no warrior, and he was uncomfortable with wars of conquest. He later objected to the annexation of Texas as a war of aggression against Mexico. He was antislavery, as his father and many of his fellow New Englanders had been. He was smart—some argue the smartest man ever to serve as president. He was depressive. He was admired by many but loved by comparatively few. He was a perfect representative of the "civilized" culture of the Northeast.

Jackson was the perfect representative of the wild southwestern frontier. In matters political and social, they were polar opposites.

Adams won their first electoral showdown. Jackson won their second. Both men fought bitterly for victory. Some call the 1828 election the most hostile, vicious election in the nation's history. Adams was quick to paint Jackson as bringing the worst extremes the frontier offered: hot temper, limited education, warrior skills but few diplomatic skills, if any. He called him a loyal son of the slave-based South. The most dangerous and contentious thing he included as a common point was that Jackson was an adulterer, and his wife a bigamist and an adulteress.

Jackson cherished his wife, Rachel, and he came from a culture that demanded he defend her. He was a duelist, who took part in at least one hundred duels during his lifetime. He had killed opponents, some for defaming Rachel's honor and reputation. He had defended her reputation throughout their years in Nashville, where increasingly civilized standards made the original self-divorce from Robards and the following elopement and unrecorded marriage increasingly scandalous to an increasingly righteous society. To have Adams make use of their past offended Jackson deeply.

In other circumstances, it is likely he would have challenged Adams to a duel, though it is less likely Adams would have accepted. In the context of an election for president of the United States, however, a duel was an impossibility. Jackson's supporters had little to fight back with. Adams was his father's son, with relatively few public vices. The campaigners claimed that Adams, during his time as ambassador to Russia, had found a prostitute for Emperor Alexander I. That sin was unproven, far away, and not a personal vice. There was little else to say. Adams was knit into a government Jackson found corrupt, but he himself was not particularly so. Jackson was forced to swallow his anger and offense.

The social strain, however, had an effect on Rachel. She suffered increasing signs of heart failure under the stress of the election. She died ten weeks before her husband was to have taken his oath of office—three weeks after his victory in the election.

Jackson never forgave Adams. In his eyes, the opposing politician had not only defamed his wife, he had murdered her. He had no realistic recourse. He never set his anger aside and never came to terms with Adams.

The Indian Removal Act of 1830

From the very start of his presidency, Andrew Jackson supported the policy of relocation of the Native Americans living in territories being filled by new European-American settlers. As the wars of Tecumseh and of the Red Shirt Creek suggested, the constant advance of European Americans into Native American territories was not going to be peaceful. While some people advocated for assimilation of "civilized" Native American tribes like the Cherokee, others were in favor of forcible reeducation of young Native Americans to make them acceptable to Euro-American society. Others continued to believe in the workability of restricting Native Americans to small reservations in their home territories, surrounded by white settlements. Many felt the simplest, most effective choice was to remove them entirely.

Jackson, having grown up on the frontier, sided with the removal policy. In his Christmas address to Congress, he

The last remaining internment fort used to imprison Cherokee people prior to their forced removal from Native lands

argued in favor of a sweeping removal of Native American tribes to the far side of the Mississippi, in the hopes that the relocation would at least buy time and separate inevitable combatants. The following year, Congress passed the Indian Removal Act of 1830. Jackson moved swiftly to implement it.

The target tribes of the Treaty were the Five Civilized Tribes of the Southern states. The tribes were the Cherokee, Choctaw, Seminole, Creek, and Chickasaw. These tribes were agricultural, and they had a government sufficiently similar in form to European rural governments that they were recognized by Euro-Americans. The Cherokee developed a unique and purely Native American form of writing, in recognition of the useful ways writing served Europeans. The members of the Five Civilized Tribes occupied land in highly valued and much-desired portions of the southwestern frontier. Perhaps worst of all, many felt that they were well suited to compete with white settlers as equals. Many held their land with full legal recognition by the local state and county governments.

This led to severe clashes between Euro-American settlers and members of the Five Civilized Tribes. Much of the problem lay in the degree to which non-Native Americans regarded land as an entitlement, for one reason or another. Some were simply racist, believing the Native Americans to be less than human—mere impediments to the manifest destiny of a new nation of European-descended Americans. Others were veterans of the Revolution and of various wars fought both before and after the establishment of the United States. Many of these veterans had been promised prime land in return for the more immediate reward of pay, and the US government was unreliable about repayment. Others were new immigrants so desperate for land, with all its economic and social prestige, that they could not endure the idea of that dream being withheld from them by people who did not seem to value the land as they did. More had lost friends and relations to various Native American uprisings or Euro-American massacres, and simply were past caring, so long as they got land, revenge, and security. Regardless of the underlying reasons, there were many white settlers who felt incapable of sharing land and land ownership with the Native American nations.

Jackson implemented his power in the new act swiftly, purchasing Native American land by eminent domain some of the time and simply removing tribe members in other instances. He pushed through a new treaty, the Treaty of New Echota, that led many Cherokee chiefs to cede their local lands and accept lands in the Midwest. There have been doubts on the legality of the Treaty of New Echota on multiple counts, including the limited rights of the signers to make such an agreement on a tribewide basis. Many Cherokee resisted the following forced eviction. All but a scattered few were rounded up and forcibly marched from their land and their homes in the southwestern frontier territories, and brought under guard to new reservations on the western side of the Mississippi.

The policy was practiced throughout both of Andrew Jackson's terms of office and continued by his successor and protégé, Martin Van Buren. The evictions of tribes occurred in waves throughout those years, some more brutal than others. Among the worst was the 1838 eviction of the Cherokee to Oklahoma. The entire process came to be called the Trail of Tears, a title that is in common use today among both Native American and Euro-American cultures. The death rates of the marches were staggering. The displacement suffered by the tribes continues to this day. The emotional costs were so great that many appear to have died of culture shock alone.

Details on Nullification

The question of slavery was a problem before the United States were even imagined. The culture and economy that developed in the Southern states to deal with a shortage of labor was entirely different from that developed by the Northern states. The cultural ideals were also different. The North was influenced by bourgeois hopes and expectations, with many of the settlers coming from common and mercantile families in trade. Their ideal was closer to a small guild town made up of local farmers, craftsmen, and tradesmen, than of anything having to do with worldly grandeur.

The South was different, investing from the start in dreams of opening up a new world grounded in the aristocratic structures of Europe at the time of the late Renaissance and early Baroque era. It was no accident that so many of the Southern colonies were named after kings and queens, or referred to them.

The South aspired to be an agricultural land of noble estates. Their ideals of government and culture, combined with their economic dependence on the slave-based model of Southern agriculture and business, made them suspicious of the federal government. The same issues that chafed them under English rule rose in relation to a federal government. Over time, the South evolved its own theories of how the balance of power in the United States was supposed to work. In their own belief and understanding, the Union functioned only to the degree the states allowed. The legislature and courts of the states had the right of nullification of laws and taxes that imposed on the states.

The idea of nullification has recurred multiple times during the history of the United States, and it remains an ideal for many in modern times. In Andrew Jackson's time, it came to a head in the early years of Jackson's presidency. In 1828, a series of tariffs was passed that was felt to work to the disadvantage of South Carolina and the Southern slave states. The North was thought to benefit, as it imported fewer foreign goods. The North was also the primary center of trade shipment, meaning that while being spared tariffs the South suffered for importing foreign goods, they profited by transporting those goods.

South Carolina raised up the possibility of invoking nullification to reject the tariffs. The turmoil continued, becoming more intense from the time the tariffs were imposed until July 14, 1832. On that date, Jackson signed the Tariff of 1832. This tariff was intended to be a compromise, modifying the terms of the first. It was hoped the compromise would satisfy South Carolina. It did not. South Carolina organized a state convention where it passed the Ordinance of Nullification, making the principle of nullification a standing part of state law.

Under Jackson's leadership, the federal government presented a two-pronged response. In one day, on March 15, 1833, Congress passed the Force Bill, granting President Jackson the right to use military force against South Carolina to maintain federal power, and also passed a new Compromise Tariff. South Carolina, when offered a choice

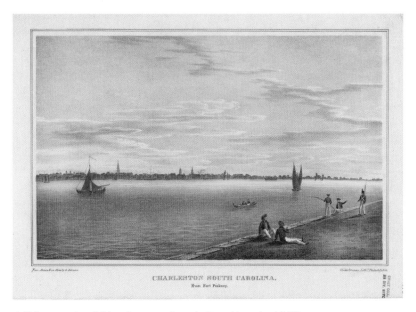

A lithograph of Charleston, South Carolina, in 1830

between the carrot and the stick, chose the carrot. They accepted the new, revised tariff and reconvened the state convention. The convention struck down the Ordinance of Nullification. Jackson had led his nation through a potential crisis that could have caused the dissolution of the Union or resulted in the Civil War being waged almost thirty years sooner than it was. The principle of nullification, however, has never entirely passed away and remains a contested approach to the government of the United States to this day.

Martin Van Buren: Unlikely Ally

During his presidency, Andrew Jackson formed a lasting alliance with Martin Van Buren, the man to follow him in the office. In many ways, Van Buren would seem an unlikely partner for Jackson. Jackson was a native of the Southern frontier. He was a fierce, direct, and blunt warrior. His loyalty to the Union was matched only by his loyalty to his culture and what he saw as his people— the hardscrabble settlers and soldiers and their equally hardscrabble women—who were filling the great American "wilderness" at a great pace.

Van Buren was a Northerner, a New Yorker of Dutch descent, and a businessman. While he did not attend college, he was solidly educated in private schools, after which he went on to apprentice in law under the supervision of two Federalist lawyers, Peter Silvester and his son. He was polished, urbane, and a political organizer to the bone. His skill as a political organizer exceeded his skill as a leader. He was a one-term president, overwhelmed by the Panic of 1837, and rejected in his second run as a result. His years of labor as a party organizer were vital in the consolidation of what became the Democratic Party, and he was of great use to Andrew Jackson.

During Jackson's election, while serving his own term as senator, he was a pivotal force organizing the consolidation of Jackson's supporters in the South and

A portrait of Martin Van Buren, by George P. A. Healy, 1858

in the mid-Atlantic states. He was diplomatic and canny. During Jackson's two terms, Van Buren became his most trusted adviser and ally. It was through Jackson's efforts that Van Buren achieved his own presidency.

He served as both secretary of state and vice president to Jackson. He proved to be a strong advisor but a weak leader. His own presidency was a crushing failure, in which crisis followed crisis, and Van Buren struggled for control. Some of the crises of his presidency included many of the worst atrocities of the Indian Removal Act; the Tariff Crisis of 1837; and dreadful mismanagement in the face of a growing Mormon faith.

After the disaster of his presidency, he returned to political organization. Secure again in his proper niche, he excelled. His role in the development of the American two-party system can't be underestimated.

BORN TO COMMAND.

A cartoon of Andrew Jackson as "King," mocking the president for tyranny against American laws and standards

OF VETO MEMORY.

HAD I BEEN CONSULTED.

VETO.

CONSTITUTION of the UNITED STATES of America

Internal Improvements U.S. Bank

KING ANDREW THE FIRST.

Hero or Villain?

Chapter Four

When we study the past, we are constantly faced with the problem that what seemed right and normal to people of another time and place can seem criminal and outrageous to modern eyes. Our time is not their time. Our moral standards are not theirs.

Evaluating a Polarizing Figure

Cambridge scholar Denys Arthur Winstanley wrote, in 1912, that "nothing is more unfair than to judge the men of the past by the ideas of the present." Few of us are able to avoid imposing modern judgment on the past. Many of us go to the past hoping to learn moral truth from history. We want to understand what was good, and what was bad, what worked, and what failed. We want to know who were the good guys and who were the bad guys, in the hope of picking the right sides in modern times. After all, "Those who fail to learn from the past are doomed to repeat it," is a much more famous quote than Winstanley's.

Often when we go back to past events and past figures, we find that the truth is unclear. When it is clear, it's morally unenlightening. It's not enough that we find it difficult to judge accurately and fairly in our own time—we often find that the people of the past found judgment just as hard.

Andrew Jackson was revered by many in his own time as a living hero and a "good guy." His actions and his principles, his courage and his military victories, his sense of his own honor and his wife's honor, even his hot temper and his acts of violence all satisfied one American notion of ideal manliness and heroism. His actions, both before he was elected president and after, filled people's hearts with pride and courage. Much like Washington before him and Lincoln after him, he was idolized and made into a legendary figure.

At the same time, there were many who considered him a monster, for many of the same actions and beliefs that made his fans and supporters raise him up as a hero.

That polarization remains true in modern times. It is almost impossible to find anyone with a neutral opinion of Andrew Jackson. To many, he's still "the People's President," or "Old Hickory." They see him as tough but fair. They see him as a hero of his nation in multiple ways, from his service during the Revolutionary War to his management of the nullification crisis, in which he succeeded in preserving the Union without having to go to war with the South. There are even many now who approve of his actions in establishing the Native American removal policies and procedures. To others, Jackson is nothing more than an imperialist conqueror, a savage colonialist, a racist biased against both Native Americans and black African and African-descended slaves, and a financial klutz of monumental proportions who appeased the South during the nullification crisis. He also introduced a form of populism to the nation based on ethnic prejudices and emotional loyalties over rational insight and diplomatic understanding.

How did Jackson come to be so polarizing? What ideas and perceptions combine to make him seem a hero to some and a villain to others? Can we reach a fair and balanced judgment about Andrew Jackson, or are we doomed to take sides?

Perception Bias

To evaluate Jackson more fairly, we first have to overcome our perception bias—the tendency for people to jump to conclusions about what data mean based on existing assumptions and expectations. We all tend to see Jackson through the veil of our own beliefs and loyalty. Our biases come into play as soon as we begin to study a person or an event.

Consider Andrew Jackson's early life and family. He was born of Scots-Irish parents. He lost his father before he was even born and was raised by his mother and close family. He had limited access to education, as we understand it in modern times. When the Revolutionary War began, he and his two elder brothers were recruited to support the American forces. His oldest brother died of heat stroke in one battle. He and his next-oldest brother were taken captive by the British in another battle. Their treatment at the hands of the British was abusive. They contracted smallpox while held captive. Their mother arranged for their release. She came to collect them and travel home on foot with them. His brother, however, was too ill and weak from his time as a British captive and died three days after their release. His mother, having taken time to nurse Andrew back to health, then volunteered to help nurse prisoners of war on ships infected with cholera. She died during her time nursing. Andrew Jackson blamed the British for his personal losses and never forgave them.

Depending on your existing biases, there are many ways you can see these facts—and these are among the least polarizing of Jackson's history. It is still possible to see him multiple ways. You can see a rough hooligan from a clannish family, coarse and uneducated, and fiercely rebellious toward the existing government. You can see a clever boy from a strong Scots-Irish family that was successful in Ireland and came to America to further their success. Struck by bad fortune and the death of her husband, his mother rallied her family, allying with close relatives. When war came, she and her sons stepped up to serve their ideals and help create a new nation.

You can see the boys as not very different from the child-soldiers of Sierra Leone, recruited young, spent easily, and brutalized by their experiences. You can also see them as patriotic young heroes doing their bit in whatever form possible.

By the standards of his culture, Andrew Jackson, his mother, and his brothers were heroes. They were strong, loyal to each other, and worked with their relatives and community to carry their own weight and hold fast as a family. They believed in liberty and the potential of a new nation and disagreed with British rule. When war came, they volunteered within the norms of that period and time. Andrew may have only been thirteen—but thirteen was considered old enough to take part in the fight for liberty in those days.

The first step when reading history is to understand what the people of the time thought they were doing, and why. You may disagree with them, but you'll learn how different systems of good and evil work.

At the same time that Andrew and his family would have considered themselves patriots and survivors, the British would have seen them as traitors and rebels, defying their lawful government. Northern patriots would have considered the family rough and uncivilized, but loyal and courageous. Neighboring Tories loyal to the British would have considered them traitors to their king, but otherwise good and resourceful members of the community. Each would bring their own standards, expectations, and judgments to the task of evaluating four people who spent most of their time simply trying to survive as a family.

Understanding how powerful biases alter how we interpret information allows us to try to compensate, stripping away the layers of our own expectations to attempt to see what kind of lives people were trying to live, and what the actual benefits and losses their actions and beliefs brought into being.

The Jacksons strengthened their community and their extended family. They survived together, in the face of great difficulty. They chose a new governmental form, and their actions helped bring about a new nation that would live using that system of government. Within the boundaries of their own lives, they were good. Others hoping for different outcomes would have disagreed. Within their own notion of good and bad, they were good people, and maybe even heroes.

The Hermitage

With all of that in mind, it's possible to consider the major concerns arising from Andrew Jackson's life and actions.

In creating and maintaining the family home and plantation at the Hermitage, Jackson behaved in a way entirely consistent with the standards of the majority of his region and his culture. The South considered the plantation as the ultimate expression of its own ideals. The plantation was a productive, agricultural, feudal estate, owned and run by an exceptional member of the South's elite. Whether by inheritance, skill, martial prowess, or business talent, the man who could successfully establish and maintain a plantation and keep control over the estate's many types of dependents fulfilled the role of "lord of the manor."

To Southerners at the time, a plantation home represented the best of European culture and history, and the virtue of a class system based on what was believed to

Tennessee Gentleman, a portrait of Andrew Jackson in retirement at the Hermitage, by Ralph E. W. Earl

be natural rank. Jackson's culture was committed to the idea that black African-descended slaves were naturally suited to servile labor, either rugged heavy labor or more refined household labor. They similarly believed that lower-class whites were naturally suited to the positions of freemen in the old feudal system, serving as managers and overseers of slaves, craftsmen, lower-level mercantile laborers, and as free farmers and sharecroppers. Most of all, they believed that the highest orders of people were naturally intended to rule, first over their estates, and then over their communities, their states, and their nation.

It was a view of the world not much different from the old European concept of the Great Chain of Being and the Divine Right of Kings. This feudal idea of how the world worked was based on the belief that God assigned people to their proper place in life. If you had been meant to be a ruler, you would have been born into a ruler's family, raised as a prince, or trained as a statesman. If you were born a peasant, you were meant to be a peasant. Everyone had their place, and the world was ordered properly. There was room for competition, but it was expected to exist largely within classes. A brewer would be admired if he struggled to become the very best brewer in his county. He was not expected to attempt to strive to become a knight. It was not just annoying if a peasant tried to try to change positions, it was a defiance of God and of the natural order. Aristocrats, most of all kings, were divinely appointed. To rebel against the rightful rule of the king was to rebel against God's own choice of ruler.

The core of this vision of the world was that people belonged in their roles through natural traits and tendencies. In the original European version, the system had only limited racial or ethnic bias. The natural prejudice of the system was aimed at class and occupation, rather than race.

It is easy to argue that common sense would show that the "natural order" was very unnatural. Millions of people through history accepted similar ranking systems and accepted them as precise descriptions of the world as it was and as it must be. If you believe that such a system is natural, proper, contributes to the order and stability of the world, and is determined by God, then it becomes both foolish and sinful to rebel against the system.

For many Southerners, a similar belief system was preached from every pulpit, announced in every scientific journal, discussed at length in newspapers, and taught in school. Within that frame of understanding, Andrew Jackson was a righteous man and a representative of what was best in Southern culture. To those who owned slaves, disciplining them seemed right and necessary. Profiting from them was the proper role and obligation of a man whose merit had made him a leader and a man of power. In this system, the slave-based estate of the Hermitage was not a sign of Jackson's moral failings, but of his natural merit and worth. It was the proper home and business of a heroic man. His experiences as a soldier, an officer, a businessman, a lawyer, and a judge further shored up the sense that Jackson was entitled to an estate of his own: it was an earned benefit of a man of great worth and usefulness to his nation.

The Great Chain of Being, an illustration of the hierarchical understanding of power and status dating back to the Middle Ages

Even at that time, there were many people, both in the Southern community and beyond, who doubted the validity of this ranking system. Many Protestants and settlers from Protestant nations believed in the value of work and thought men and women should be ambitious beyond their "natural" class and rank. Others were influenced by Enlightenment philosophy and reasoning, which rejected the notion of a meddling, interfering God in favor of a clockmaker God who, having set the universe going like a wind-up watch, sat back and allowed humans to interact with free will. Others, drawn from the rapidly rising mercantile classes of England, the Netherlands, and the various German nations, took their understanding of life's natural order from their understanding of trade and of those who succeeded in trade. This group associated financial success with proper living choices. They were the first to explore what is now called "The Prosperity Gospel," and they were more likely to declare the divine right of the successful merchant than they were to accept the divine right of kings. Each of these traditions was present in both the new United States as a whole, and the Northern states in particular. Together, they blended to form a meritocracy-based culture that valued the free man and woman, believed the laborer was worth his or her hire, and that men and women, through thrift and hard work, could rise in both the world and in God's eyes.

In the eyes of many from these traditions, the Southern ideals of the slave-run plantation and the elite plantation owner were obscene and ungodly. The ownership of slaves was against God's own will, though many believed God approved of many other, equally horrifying things.

People of this tradition would have admired Jackson for his rugged, hard-working, deprived childhood, his work to rise above his station, his military heroism, his public service, and his financial success. They would not have approved of his plantation or slaves, and would not have believed them to reflect the natural order of the world.

Using these two frames to evaluate the same information, it's possible to see Andrew Jackson as either a hero and a highly successful man enjoying the reward for his merit, or a man of skill and worth, falling into sin and decadence as a result of indulging in a lifestyle based on the abuse of other humans.

Modern people, judging the issue of slavery in the South and the existence of plantations like the Hermitage, draw in some cases on these old cultural tropes. As often, though, we frame our judgements in terms of evolutionary science, sociology, and statistics.

These tools can be used and abused by almost any faction, arguing almost any position. Many people who believe in the equality of humans draw their belief from genetic and evolutionary material that show there is very little genetic difference between racial groups, and that those differences have very little clear effect on intelligence, skills, morals, or ability to behave lawfully. Other groups who believe passionately will draw on the same tools, if not always the same data, to prove the reverse, arguing that there are deep differences between racial groups that suggest the races should naturally be treated differently.

Damage: The Battle of Horseshoe Bend

There are many other approaches to making a fair evaluation of historical figures. You can try to weigh the good accomplished by an action against the damage done. Consider the Battle of Horseshoe Bend.

It's clear that the Red Stick faction of the Creek nation was trying to gather the rest of the Creek to go to war with the Euro-American settlers in and around their territory. In the process, they were triggering a civil war among the Creek nation, while forging strong political alliances with Tecumseh's Shawnee in Ohio and along the United States' northern frontier boundary.

The basis for choosing to fight would meet many of the standards we currently believe define a just war, or a moral war. Their land was being invaded, their people were being murdered, and their economic system was being destroyed through interaction with the Euro-American trade system. The settlers were bringing in new diseases that were more dangerous to the Native Americans than to immigrant groups. The invaders refused to reliably deal with the Natives. Both individuals and the many levels of government felt free to break treaties and contracts with Native Americans, to cheat them in business dealings, and to deny them fair treatment in the courts when they attempted to find legal remedies for these problems. Euro-American use of land ruined it for traditional Native use. In a matter of roughly

An etching of the Battle of
Horseshoe Bend, 1814

two centuries, the newcomers had gone from a small, largely helpless, impoverished group to a mighty force so powerful it was already uncertain whether there was anything the Native Americans could accomplish by resisting.

If the Red Sticks began a war, first among themselves and then with the United States, there would be enormous damage and loss of life. It would not matter who won; the damage would be enormous. Both sides had the will and the ability to slaughter each other in huge numbers. In the process, both cultures would have been damaged on all levels.

Andrew Jackson and his troops ended the Creek War in one encounter. Their actions prevented the Red Stick faction from obtaining any of the advantages they hoped to gain from a war—a result benefiting Euro-Americans and non–Red Stick Creeks. They also prevented the Red Sticks from inflicting the damage they hoped to inflict on Euro-American settlers. The alliances with Tecumseh and other border tribes were disrupted. Jackson killed over eight hundred Native Americans. He lost less than fifty of his own soldiers.

By almost any scale, the damage done was less than the damage prevented. One can argue that it is unfair that things had reached a point where the Native Americans could not hope to recover their former power and position without waging a great war among themselves and with their invaders. That would be true. It would not change the fact that Jackson's actions saved many lives on both sides of the conflict and served to prevent an even larger conflict from developing.

In this situation, it is possible to argue that Jackson was a hero. Assessment of damage and of benefit can help avoid problems like personal motives and cultural expectations. In this kind of evaluation, a hero does more good than damage, and a villain does more damage than good.

That leaves out crucial questions that often matter as much or more than just pro and con or profit and loss. Did Andrew Jackson respect his enemies? Did he act out of bigotry? Was he acting to promote imperial or colonialist goals? Did he act in hate or in charity?

People with heroic hearts and virtuous intentions can do horrible damage. People with villainous ambitions and cold motives can do great good, benefiting everyone around them. Which is more important? What matters more, intentions or results?

Self-Interest vs. Altruism; The Indian Removal Act

Another standard to apply when evaluating whether someone is a hero or a villain may be a judgment of who profits. Is the act one of self-interest or of altruism?

Andrew Jackson, in his first address to Congress, begged for the House of Representatives to pass an act allowing Jackson to purchase Native American lands in territories that were already largely occupied by Euro-Americans, or which were intensely desired by Euro-Americans. In return, the Native Americans would be given lands on the western side of the Mississippi that would, hypothetically, be reserved for them and for their use from then on. He also

A bronze statue commemorating the Trail of Tears, in Pulaski, Tennessee

asked for the right to remove Native Americans by force. Congress granted Jackson his wish in the spring of 1830. The atrocities that followed over the next decade and more are now known as the "Trail of Tears." Members of many Native American nations lost their lands, saw their cultures destroyed, and discovered that no treaty could be trusted. Thousands of men, women, and children died. The wealth of a people was cast aside or stolen from the Native tribes by Euro-Americans. Andrew Jackson's reasons for requesting the Indian Relocation Act may have been altruistic in spite of the outcome. In the words of thousands of people over hundreds of years, "he meant well."

To understand Jackson's concerns, it's important to remember the reasoning behind his actions at the Battle of Horseshoe Bend. The hope was to end the possibility of the Red Stick Creek to wage civil war on their own people, or a war of defense against Euro-American settlers. The reasons were that the damage likely to occur vastly outweighed any benefit either side might reasonably hope to gain from outright war. A long-term war between Natives and settlers along the border stretching from the Gulf of Mexico to the Great Lakes would have been catastrophic to both sides.

Such wars were brewing all along that border, within the United States and its territories. They were developing even in territories not yet fully explored, as rumor and reporting passed from tribe to tribe. The balance between the United States and the Native American tribes had reached a critical point at which outright war could only bring disaster down on everyone. There were far too many Euro-American citizens of the United States to simply chase away, or even massacre easily. The new nation had a technological advantage, through its efficient farming, manufacturing, and trading abilities. The United States had weapons, supplies, and a deep and abiding determination to remain in the New World—the land of the free or the land of their destiny.

The Native Americans would not and could not easily move either. They had nowhere to go. Their homes and their history were there in their territories. Their cultures were already in crisis. Their war was just, and their need was enormous.

Neither Native Americans nor settlers could be counted on to have the wisdom not to act like feuding neighbors. Both Natives and settlers had set off brutal conflicts during their short history together. It took only one person with a weapon and a grudge to start an uprising.

Jackson faced a situation more volatile than a shed full of gunpowder and a thousand people tossing lit matches. An uprising could quickly consolidate both sides, raising determination to fight to the bitter end.

Many settlers, when they argued Native Americans and settlers could not live together peacefully, intended the comment as an insult to Native Americans. Others, however, meant it as an assessment of the inherent conflicts between the two cultures. They were at odds, and neither side would easily give in. If nothing else, no one was really in control. Euro-Americans could not stop the constant flood of incoming settlers from overseas—there were just too many Europeans desperate for freedom, land, and opportunity.

News of the Indian Removal Act is read to the Cherokee.

The explorers of the sixteenth century had opened a tap that could not be closed again. The tribes could not be easily controlled either, and their anger and desperation were entirely reasonable.

From Jackson's point of view, the only option was to separate the combatants, giving the Euro-Americans the land they coveted and attempting to offer some degree of recompense to the evicted tribes. That is not to say Jackson felt a deep affection or any great charity toward the Native tribes. He was a child of the frontier, and a soldier experienced in the Native American wars. He was, in the end, loyal to his own people first. There is no indication, however, that his decision to back Native American removal was malicious. Jackson, like many, appears to have thought it the best option available that could be managed in the time left.

Was he a hero? There are many who think his actions probably prevented a war. Some believe that the tribes exiled would have ended up slaughtered outright or absorbed entirely if they had stayed. It was, in the end, done in service to Jackson's side more than out of altruism toward the Native Americans. Most of all, it was done to avoid a worse outcome. Considering how bad the Native American removals were, that's not saying too much, but it was better than it could have been.

Does that make Jackson a hero, a villain, or simply a pragmatic politician, making the best choice he saw available? It's not always possible to do good. It's not even always possible to avoid evil. How do we judge the man who does both good and evil?

Nullification

The final point to consider in evaluating Jackson as a hero or a villain is the subject of nullification, and the actions he took to keep South Carolina from attempting that policy. Jackson's actions avoided civil war. Through actions he requested of Congress, he established the legal right of the federal government to use force to deal with any state attempting to deny the federal government final, primary power. At the exact same time, he backed down on the federal government's imposed taxation on a bitterly unwilling state, and readjusted law to lend more favor to the slave-based economies of the South.

Jackson preserved the Union—and also preserved the slave-based economic system. He drew a military line in the sand. He also avoided acting on that limit, instead backing down to the demands South Carolina was making. He caved in to pressure from the slave-owning states.

Jackson had been born, lived, and died in South Carolina and Tennessee. He was a superb example of what the South valued in a man. He was a plantation owner and a slave owner. His sympathies in regards to the institution of slavery and the plantation system were evident. However, he was at odds with his own culture regarding nullification. He believed in the necessity of federal power to hold and govern the Union, and he believed passionately in the need to preserve the Union.

His actions can be seen as an expression of both beliefs. He gave in to South Carolina's demands and allowed the slave economy to survive and to maintain power over the

The Founding Fathers, including Jefferson (*second from left*), discussing core ideals

Union … but he was a slave owner himself. He resisted the threat to the Union, though, which he saw as unacceptable.

In the end, he merely delayed the Civil War. Appeasement of the Southern states would become increasingly impossible over time. There were only two possible outcomes, both obtained through war: a divided country or a Union maintained by force. Yet Jackson can't be held responsible for failing to see the Civil War was inevitable. Within the framework of his time and culture, he took action that allowed that threat to pass in his time, on his watch. Both the threat of force and the appeasement of South Carolina helped bring that about. Jackson's actions saved his nation, and his time, from conflict.

Thomas Jefferson

We are living in a time that is quick to judge and slow to consider. We have come to regret many of the actions of our ancestors, but few of us understand their world well enough to know how they may have avoided the mistakes they made. More and more often, we hold historical figures to standards we ourselves could not have sustained in the same place and time. We struggle when it comes to particularly well-loved and admired legends of our past.

As a diplomat, a politician, and a philosopher, Thomas Jefferson is central to our modern sense of our nation's ideals and goals. Whether we are quoting from the Declaration of Independence or the Constitution, we are overwhelmed by Jefferson's vision of what our nation and our people could become. If he had only added one sentence to the hundreds he gave our nation, he would still have gifted us with a brilliant statement of what has become a core American value:

"We hold these truths to be self-evident, that all men are created equal, that they are endowed by their Creator with certain unalienable Rights, that among these are the Life, Liberty and the Pursuit of Happiness."

Jefferson was among those who helped negotiate a political compromise with the Southern states, preserving the institution of slavery. He himself was a slave owner. Worse, he took a slave as a lover, fathering children with her, when she had neither the power nor the legal right to object. By the standards of modern Americans, his actions were both hypocritical and abusive.

How are we to judge Thomas Jefferson? How can we balance his failings and his greatness? Which is more important—that he imagined the possibility that all men were created equal, or that he failed to respect that equality in his slaves? How can we assess a man who recognized that England was abusing its power over its colonial subjects, who could not legally resist the laws passed regarding them, but failed to recognize that it was abusive to take a woman as a lover when she had no power or leverage to protest?

Jefferson's vision was part and parcel of the changes that brought about the Civil War, freed the slaves, empowered the civil rights movement, and brought us to modern day, when we consider our slave-owning ancestors and cringe. It was his vision of what America could be, more than any other, that has inspired our generations to improve. It was also Jefferson who sold out the slaves to make an expedient political deal with other slave owners.

In the end, the most honest thing to do may be to accept that all men and women are stained by the time in which they live and unlikely to resist all the various corruptions their own eras considered normal. Any other answer forces us to denounce virtually all our greatest leaders for failing to overcome their own times ... and to know that, in our own future, someone will be forced to denounce us in turn for acts we ourselves cannot yet recognize as wrong.

Andrew Jackson served as
president from 1829 to 1837.

Summing It Up

So—was Andrew Jackson a hero, or a villain? Was he a great president who led our nation through difficult times to safe harbors, or was he a hypocrite and a moral failure who added some of the darkest stains to America's history?

Overview

Before all, Jackson was a man of his time and of his culture. He was the child of Scots-Irish parentage raised among family members on the Southern frontier. He was raised in a society that blended the standards of the Scots-Irish with the native-born settlers, and modified both to adjust to the conditions on the frontier. The territory was dangerous. The communities were at risk from natural disaster and from conflict of many sorts. Men and women were both expected to be industrious, strong, loyal to kin and to neighbors, and capable of not only looking after themselves, but also contributing to the community's security.

Jackson grew up with many challenges. His father died before he was even born. He was brought up by his mother, in the home of relatives. He and his two elder brothers had access to education, but not to extended or exceptional schooling. They lived in a working community and would have been expected to carry their own weight.

Jackson appeared to have accepted the social standards of his community. He was extremely conscious of his personal honor and that of his wife. He was a willing fighter. He was also a willing duelist, killing some of his opponents. He fought over a hundred duels during his lifetime, many over the honor of his wife, Rachel. He does not appear to have felt substantial remorse or regret over his duels or over opponents who died. Instead, he accepted duels as acts that were necessary to defend his and Rachel's honor. While he was a willing duelist and a murderer by today's standards, he was not undisciplined. He could hate someone like John Quincy Adams with a deep and lasting passion without being foolish enough to attempt to kill him. By the standards of his own era, he was not a murderer, following the rules laid down and the code of the duel.

He was a patriot to his newly established nation. He was a hard-working man. Within the expectations of his culture, he was ethical; it should be recognized that his culture appreciated an astute man, however, on the battlefield, in business, and in conflicts with others. While he was canny in his business dealings, he was not corrupt, and he fought corruption in government during his terms of office.

He accepted the imperial ideals of his nation and was comfortable with the notion of gaining territory through military conquest. He was not uncomfortable with the expectation that the United States would grow, occupying land formerly held by the Native American tribes and nations. He was capable of admiring the Native Americans but equally capable of manipulating them. He was able to hope for Native Americans to be assimilated while advancing a policy of removal separating them from white society. He appears to have been at ease with both his time fighting the Natives in the Indian Wars and with the outcome of the Indian Removal Act.

In the same way, he was comfortable with the slavery of the Southern states. He and his wife owned slaves and used slaves as a primary source of labor on their plantation. His treatment of his slaves appeared to have been generally good, within limits. Unfortunately, those limits include an expectation that slaves be disciplined with physical punishment. A study of the buildings of the Hermitage suggest he housed his slaves well and fed them appropriately. The testimony of one of his slaves, Hannah, indicated he maintained a paternal relationship with his slaves. There is no sign that he objected to the slave system on any level, and as president, he worked to ensure the slave states could maintain their status.

He served his nation for virtually his entire adult life. He was recruited into combat as a young boy. He was a courier during the Revolutionary War. He was a captive of the British. He lost both his elder brothers and his mother to that war. He repeatedly served in the Tennessee militia and the federal army, going up against enemies both foreign and domestic. He also served in nonmilitary capacities, as prosecutor and judge, as well as serving as a congressman and a senator, and as president.

Evaluation

Jackson's life shows little indication that he ever wished to be a criminal or a villain. His intentions were as positive as one can normally expect and were far more admirable than those of many people alive today. He wished to do good in the world, to serve and protect his nation and his loved ones. He wished to prosper, in a time and place where prosperity was considered an admirable goal. Judged on intention alone, there is every reason to consider Jackson a hero. He was brave, valiant, dedicated, and gave most of his life to some form of service. He was a faithful spouse. He and his wife failed to have children, but he adopted two sons willingly and appeared to have been a good father to both—not only to his wife's nephew, but to the Creek boy he adopted. Within the limits of his culture and society, he was a great man, and very much the sort of man his culture admired.

Jackson was absolutely accepting of what might best be considered the villainy of his culture, though. He accepted the practice of dueling. He accepted the intentional ongoing conflict with the Native Americans and the willing theft

The Revolutionary War had an impact on Jackson's life and career.

of their lands. He accepted slavery. He accepted shrewd trading in land deals—another form of theft from the Native Americans. As important as his honor and his wife's honor were to him, he was nonetheless willing to shortcut the divorce process and disregard her former husband, and to risk their reputations by taking the frontier route of self-divorce and questionably legal marriage, rather than arrange for a fully legal, aboveboard divorce and marriage. He does not appear to have deeply questioned the beliefs and convictions of his own society.

The outcomes of his actions were varied. The result of his shortcut marriage to Rachel was a lifetime of insults, scandals, duels, and rejections. He married Rachel sooner by cutting corners, but he appears to have lost her sooner, also, in direct connection with the stress of his election, when her adultery and bigamy were publicly aired and used against him. Her heart attack mere weeks after Jackson's election victory was brought about by the shame and strain of the election, in his mind. There is no reason to doubt it did have an effect, though it seems likely she suffered from some underlying heart disease also.

He caused damage as a soldier and as a statesman. Whether considering Native Americans dead in battle or Native Americans dead as a result of forced eviction from their own homelands, there were many who died unnecessarily. If the underlying reason for his actions was misplaced faith in the righteousness of his own culture, it does not undo the damage done. In the same way, his belief

A stately portrait of Andrew Jackson

in the slave system and the reasoning used to support it do not absolve him of the damage done to over one hundred slaves who lived in bondage to a master who was known to flog slaves for discipline.

By these standards, Jackson was a villain—but he was not a personal villain. He was a socially brainwashed villain causing damage and pain out of complete belief that his culture endorsed good behaviors.

There is a moral difference between someone who does evil by intent and someone who does evil out of misplaced faith—in a bad leader, a bad cultural norm, or a bad religious principle. Andrew Jackson was not a willing villain in any sense, but he behaved villainously under the influence of his culture's beliefs. He was a hero by intention and in many cases a hero by courage, honor, and by end results. He was a villain by allowing systemic villainy to lead him into evil behavior.

A Final Overview

When studying figures and events in the past, it can be difficult to get past our own cultural beliefs and assumptions to evaluate who was a hero and who was a villain. We can't make a fair case without setting aside our own assumptions and testing the facts as they come in. As satisfying as it can be to declare that this character is a despicable imperialist or an anti-Semite, another a racist, or yet another a committed misogynist, the values of our own time tell us more about ourselves than they do about those who lived in the past. We have come very far from our ancestors' cultures, but we cannot know which of our beliefs will prove as mistaken as the beliefs of slave owners, who believed themselves natural rulers of an inferior race.

It is equally important to recognize that some villainy is not personal or even intended, but is systemic. There are few, if any, who entirely escape each and every villainy of their culture. Some taint of the times seems inevitable.

It is important that we refuse to absolve ourselves or our ancestors too quickly. Systemic villainy is not necessarily intended, or even understood, but the results are just as evil. If Andrew Jackson had sought a different answer to the encroaching violence between Native Americans and land-greedy settlers, or if he had implemented his Indian Removal Act with more oversight and compassion—if he had questioned his own cultural beliefs in what could practically be done under the circumstances—the evil of the Trail of Tears might have been reduced or even eliminated. If he had resisted the lure of the slave owner's system, he could have at least reduced the harm he did, personally, in the name of slavery. But it is just as important to recognize that we are all caught in the evils of our own time … and few will dramatically overcome that evil.

In the end, it is important to recognize the greatness of our flawed historical figures, while refusing to turn a blind eye to their villainy, whether that villainy is intentional or entirely controlled by their cultural assumptions. Change only comes when people question their assumptions, and those who do are heroes of their own times.

ascendancy The term for Protestant English and Scottish settlers moved into Northern Ireland to control and stabilize the Catholic nation.

colonialist One who believes that it is appropriate and even necessary for nations to colonize territories outside their own borders.

election Selection of someone to fill a position by vote.

feudal A governmental system based on an aristocratic hierarchy of nobles and military leaders, in control of land and a supporting population of commoners.

genocide Conquest achieved by killing entire cultural or genetic groups.

imperialist One who believes that it is appropriate and even admirable for a culture to absorb other existing nations and political units through military conquest, trade conquest, or treaty, bringing them under the governmental control of an empire.

land speculation Dealing in land for profit. The term implies a much higher degree of risk and uncertainty than simple real estate deals, and is often semi-criminal.

mercantile Anything having to do with merchant trading.

Glossary

meritocracy A system in which advancement is gained through skill and competence, rather than through other methods such as nepotism, bribery, or blackmail.

militia A military or paramilitary organization run on a nonfederal level.

nullification The theory that power in the United States is ultimately vested in the states, rather than in the federal government, and that the states had the right to overturn legislation and taxation they found disadvantageous.

populism A system in which almost everybody is considered necessary and desirable members of the voting franchise, or are in some other way empowered to act within government structures.

Roanoke An early settlement in Virginia that disappeared between one contact from its suppliers and another.

Scots-Irish A group of people descended mostly from Protestant Scots and Northern English ancestors who were brought to Ireland to serve.

self-divorce The practice in frontier communities to dissolve a marriage by mutual agreement.

1767
Andrew Jackson is born.

1779–1781
Andrew's brother Hugh dies in Revolutionary War; Andrew serves in Revolutionary War and is imprisoned by the British; his older brother Robert dies.

1794
Andrew Jackson and Rachel Donelson Robards get married, which is later challenged by her former husband.

1814
Jackson signs the Treaty of Fort Jackson at the end of the Creek War.

1815
Jackson is victorious at the Battle of New Orleans.

Chronology

1828
Jackson's wife dies.

1829
Jackson is inaugurated into
the presidency.

1830
Jackson signs the newly passed
Indian Removal Act.

1833
The Force Bill and Compromise Tariff are passed;
Jackson gives his second Inaugural Address.

1845
Jackson dies at age seventy-eight.

Books

Brady, Patricia. *A Being So Gentle: The Frontier Love Story of Rachel and Andrew Jackson*. New York: St. Martin's Press, 2011.

Brands, H. W. *Andrew Jackson: His Life and Times*. New York: Anchor Books, 2006.

Meacham, Jon. *American Lion: Andrew Jackson in the White House*. New York: Random House, 2008.

Sellers, Charles. *The Market Revolution: Jacksonian America, 1815-1846*. Oxford, UK: Oxford University Press, 1994.

Watson, Harry L. *Liberty and Power: The Politics of Jacksonian America*. New York: Hill and Wang, 2006.

Wilentz, Sean. *Andrew Jackson: The American President Series: The 7th President, 1829 – 1837*. New York: Times Books, Henry Holt and Company, BCE Edition, 2007.

Videos

Jacksonian America

https://www.youtube.com/watch?v=qrc7rUM_JRc
This is a video pertaining to Jacksonian America.

JB Presents Jefferson and Jackson:
A Comparison of Visions

https://www.youtube.com/watch?v=QdnsYJf6ce4
This video discusses the differences between Jefferson and Jackson.

Websites

Jacksonian Democracy

http://www.history.com/topics/jacksonian-democracy
The History Channel's information and videos about Jacksonian democracy.

U.S. History: The Age of Jackson

http://www.ushistory.org/us/24c.asp
This page addresses the South Carolina nullification controversy.

"American Presidents Series: Andrew Jackson Biography." YouTube, March 11, 2014. https://www.youtube.com/watch?v=2MVRD6fhKUA&t=6s&index=3&list=PLvNUq3RQ0GZewRdquTZ3d-NJhpfZpYyI.

"Andrew Jackson." Biography.com, April 27, 2017. https://www.biography.com/people/andrew-jackson-9350991.

"Andrew Jackson: Facts, Information and Articles About Andrew Jackson, the 7th US President." HistoryNet, accessed November 20, 2017. http://www.historynet.com/andrew-jackson.

"Andrew Jackson: Farewell Address, March 4, 1837." The American Presidency Project, accessed November 20, 2017 http://www.presidency.ucsb.edu/ws/?pid=67087.

"Andrew Jackson – Good Evil & The Presidency – PBS Documentary." YouTube, June 11, 2012. https://www.youtube.com/watch?v=EGfxyeuy8u8&t=1609s&index=4&list=PLvNUq3URQ0GZewRdquTZ3d-NJhpfZpYyI.

"Andrew Jackson the Napoleon of America." YouTube, September 14, 2013. https://www.youtube.com/watch?v=JM-V7PgCV4A&list=PLbrekueHd3dqYc8URgmTPaF8iN0Qp1Ywg.

"Andrew Jackson: Tough As Old Hickory." Andrew Jackson's Hermitage, accessed November 20, 2017 https://thehermitage.com/learn/andrew-jackson.

Cheathem, Mark R. "Hannah, Andrew Jackson's Slave." *Humanities*, March/April 2014. https://www.neh.gov/humanities/2014/marchapril/feature/hannah-andrew-jacksons-slave.

Fischer, David Hackett. *Albion's Seed: Four British Folkways in America (America: A Cultural History)*. Oxford, UK: Oxford University Press, 1989.

Foner, Eric and John A Garraty, eds. "American-Indian Wars." In *The Reader's Companion to American History*. New York: Houghton Mifflin Harcourt Publishing Company, 1991. http://www.history.com/topics/native-american-history/american-indian-wars.

"The Greatest Land Deal in History: The Louisiana Purchase and the Destiny of America (2003)." YouTube, April 2, 2016. https://www.youtube.com/watch?v=JDPhh7Ot1tw.

Green, John. "Age of Jackson: Crash Course US History #14." YouTube, May 9, 2013. https://www.youtube.com/watch?v=beN4qE-e5O8.

Griffin, Patrick. *The People with No Name: Ireland's Ulster Scots, America's Scots Irish, and the Creation of a British Atlantic World*. Princeton, NJ: Princeton University Press, 2001.

"Indian Wars Time Table." United States History, accessed November 20, 2017. http://www.u-s-history.com/pages/h1008.html.

Kukla, Jon. *A Wilderness So Immense: The Louisiana Purchase and the Destiny of America*. New York: Anchor, 2004.

Miller Center of Public Affairs, University of Virginia. "Andrew Jackson." Accessed November 18, 2017. https://millercenter.org/president/jackson.

"Should We Judge People of Past Eras for Moral Failings?" BBC, August 20, 2013. http://www.bbc.com/news/magazine-23772194.

Sutcliffe, Thomas. "You can't judge the past by today's standards." *Independent*, January 6, 2009. http://www.independent.co.uk/voices/columnists/Thomas-sutcliffe/tom-sutcliffe-you-cant-judge-the-past-by-todays-standards-1228169.html.

Warren, Wendy. *New England Bound: Slavery and Colonization in Early America*. New York: Liveright, 2017.

Watson, Harry. "Andrew Jackson, America's Original Anti-Establishment Candidate." *Smithsonian*, March 31, 2016. https://www.smithsonianmag.com/history/andrew-jackson-americas-original-anti-establishment-candidate-180958621.

Index

Peg Robinson is a writer and editor specializing in researched educational materials and white papers. She graduated from the University of California at Santa Barbara in 2008, with honors, and attended Pacifica Graduate Institution. She served for two years as a docent for Opus Archives, focusing on converting historically significant audio recordings to digital format, securing valuable material in a less fragile recording medium. She lives in Rhode Island, with her daughter and her cat and dog.